How to Draw

Thanksgiving
Things

For Jesse, Jasmine, Justin, Jordan, Melina, and Matthew

Published in the United States of America by The Child's World®
1980 Lookout Drive • Mankato, MN 56003-1705
800-599-READ • www.childsworld.com

Acknowledgments
Illustration and Design: Rob Court
Production: The Creative Spark, San Juan Capistrano, CA

Registration

Library of Congress Cataloging-in-Publication Data
Court, Rob, 1956–
  How to draw Thanksgiving things / by Rob Court.
     p. cm. — (Doodle books)
  ISBN 978-1-59296-957-9 (library bound : alk. paper)
 1. Thanksgiving Day in art—Juvenile literature. 2. Drawing—Technique—Juvenile literature. I. Title. II. Series.

NC825.T48C68 2008
743'.893942649—dc22

2007013395

The Scribbles Institute ™

How to Draw

Thanksgiving
Things

by Rob Court

The
Child's
World

leaves

1

2

3

4

pumpkin

1

2

3

4

mashed potatoes

1

2

3

4

1

2

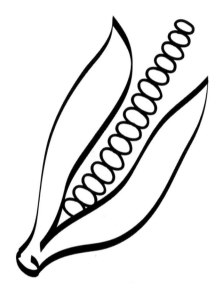

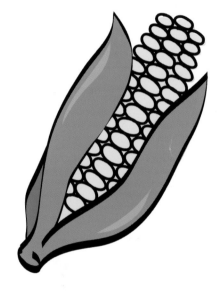

3

4

candle

1

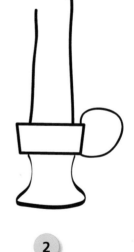

2

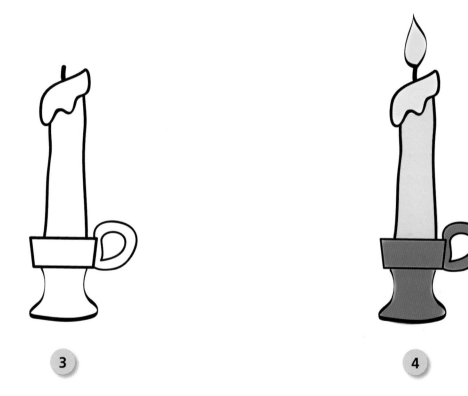

3

4

stuffing

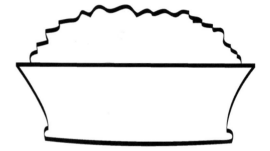

1

2

pumpkin pie

1

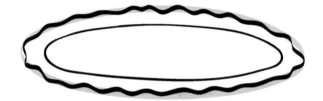

2

3

cranberries

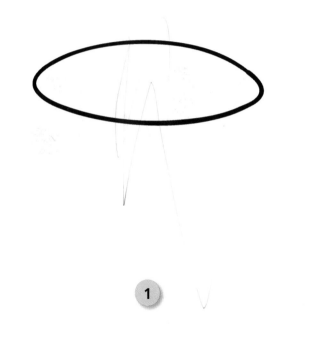

1

2

3

4

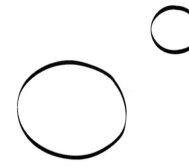

1

2

3

4

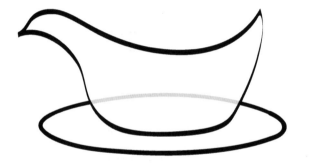

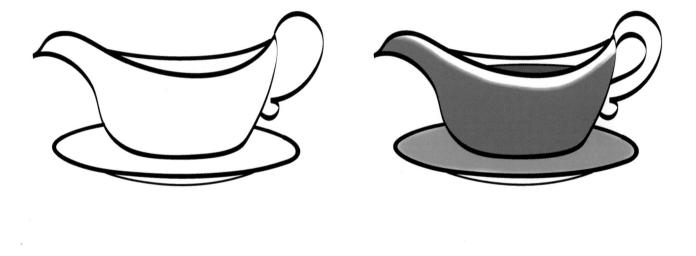

3

4

Mayflower

1

2

3

4

Pilgrim

1

2

3

4

Native American

1

2

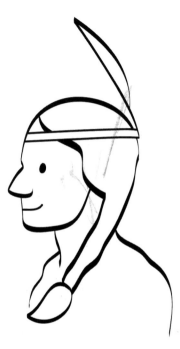

3

4

Pilgrim dress

1

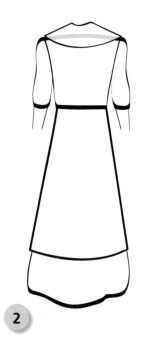

2

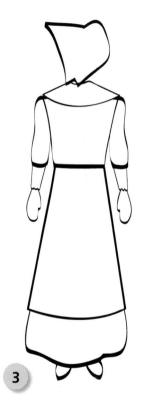

3

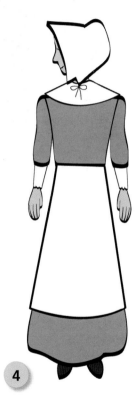

4

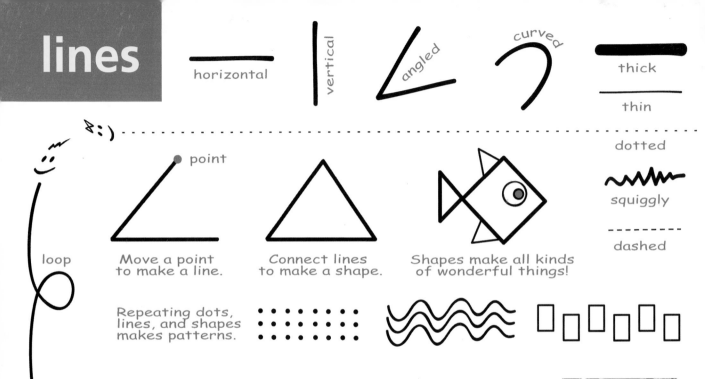

lines

horizontal

vertical

angled

curved

thick

thin

dotted

squiggly

dashed

loop

point

Move a point to make a line.

Connect lines to make a shape.

Shapes make all kinds of wonderful things!

Repeating dots, lines, and shapes makes patterns.

About the Author

Rob Court is a graphic artist and illustrator. He started the Scribbles Institute to help students, parents, and teachers learn about drawing and visual art. Please visit www.scribblesinstitute.com